Cyanometer

poems by

Faith Paulsen

Finishing Line Press
Georgetown, Kentucky

Cyanometer

ACKNOWLEDGMENTS

The author would like to thank the editors of the following publications in
which versions of some of the poems first appeared:

Cahoodaloodaling: Senior Citizens at the Retirement Center Discuss John
Ashbery's "More Reluctant"
Soul Lit: Lancaster County Pastoral, In the Night
One Art: Mother-in-Law, My Mother's Pessary
Rhythm & Versa Salon: Attention
Psaltery & Lyre: Carotenoid
https://psalteryandlyre.org/2020/09/21/carotenoid/
Seaborne: Letter to Marianas Trench
Schuylkill Valley Journal: Last Visit with Kathy

I'd like to thank the many teachers and friends who have supported me on
my poetic journey. You mean more to me than I can say.

Thanks to loved ones who have been my inspiration, including my children
Paz, Seth, and Gideon, my husband Barton Sacks, my brother and sister, and
all our parents.

Publisher: Leah Huete de Maines
Editor: Christen Kincaid
Cover Art: Cathleen Cohen
Author Photo: Gideon Paulsen-Sacks
Cover Design: Elizabeth Maines McCleavy

Order online: www.finishinglinepress.com
also available on amazon.com

Author inquiries and mail orders:
Finishing Line Press
PO Box 1626
Georgetown, Kentucky 40324
USA

Table of Contents

For "all of us"

Lancaster County Pastoral

Close so close to the road I'm jogging
the team of four horses, with Amish men in straw hats,
mow the fields for silo filling.
Wagon wheels turn the whir of the blade.
Tall cornstalks undulate, ripple, surrender,
tassles fall trembling into the wagon's deep bed.
Their work stirs up a whirlwind of leaves
wiffits of air close to my cheek
applause, silk, husk, wing, thorax,
confusion of blue black heads and forked tails
dozens of barn swallows
crossfire around me *ping ping ping*
snatching grasshoppers mid-air.
One swallow's flight
grainy ovation, its feathers swept back,
like a shot
grazes my ear.

Minnows

This is no time to be strong.
Every day we cringe.
We count our losses on our fingers
our tongues
the edges of our teeth,
in the gut, in the cowering
root, in broken pottery
and in the shards of days.
Another and another, *No, not*
another. The numbers mount up
become a forest of figures
an aggregate of violated
symbols. Our homes subjected to
uninvited guests: stinkbug, lanternfly,
elm borer, bushfire,
pandemic, lawlessness, flood.
We search the Lost and Found
not knowing which is which.
We feel each tear in our bodies
all too vividly
in colors too bright, an openness that links
lungs to throat to lips once fragrant and hungry
naked now, dried and worried, carried
like weight.
Losses swim away
like minnows
as we try to count them.

Letter to Marianas Trench

You try your best. Mind
your own briny business, tend
your own deep-sea gardens.
You hope to stay out of trouble,
not make waves. Keep your head down
and profile low. Seven miles deep—
How could you camouflage any better,
clad in thunderstorms, the Pacific
a soundproof shell, your castle a deep chasm
in the shadows of ocean?
Geothermal vents outpour
minerals frothy and hot
while in darkness kiwa crabs
wave their claws, dance
in the flow of methane
and hydrogen sulfide.
You never asked to be discovered.
What you want
is your privacy. Your currents and eddies wash
the world's impurities away, your swaying tubeworms
and pink vent fish, your snails and octopus free
from corruption.
No home is more remote, detached
from the distant compounds
where we the landlorn lug home
our desiccated spoils
in flimsy translucent wrappers.
Even now you churn and boil yourself clean.
Your cloistered populations feed on each other.
Then—despite your best efforts
a hideous dome clanks into the garden
and stares down your innocents.
They call it a record-setting dive,
a great exploration. Still, it turns out,
like Leif Erikson, a stray Dorito bag
got there first.

Mother-in-Law

Invited to call her Mom, silently I called her Umbrella in Sunshine
Flea-Market Wristwatch   Three Phone Calls A Day
Flash Flood Warning.
Why take a chance?
The cat will suck the breath out of the baby.
Spare Room Hoarder of get-well cards and flashlights
bottles of sleeping pills. *(They're not habit-forming—I should know,*
I've been taking them for years.)
She called me Broken Eggs   Hamster in a Plastic Ball.
Half-hour Early/Ten Minutes Late
She called me Barefoot in Snow—
That name I kept.
Years after her death
I wake   stunned
when others call me Worry and I respond *Be Safe.*
Please don't do
anything stupid.
Call it Poetic Justice. Call me, So soon?
I call myself, I Didn't Know—

In 1789, a scientist invented

the cyanometer, an instrument to measure the blueness of the sky:
a spinning wheel of pigments starting with white, circling to black,
52 distinct tints of Prussian blue, from skylight stone to indigo.
I want one. To calculate the spectrum
from Mary and Mohammed to Krishna, Miles Davis, Bobby Blue
Bland,
from lapis lazuli, ultramarine to pitch,
want to quantify, match the sky to the numbers.
Yesterday a wash of 4 streaked with 19,
this morning a dome of pure 22.
I want to dip my finger in distilled clouds
to test the color of your love.

I want to taste your color, dip my finger in clouds.
This morning a dome, pure 22,
tomorrow's forecast: clouds of 9, shadows of 36.
Face the sun's opposite, match the numbers to the heavens.
Pitch, lapis lazuli, ultramarine,
52 tints of Prussian blue from indigo stone to the light of the sky.
My want, calibrated in the cones of my eyes
all of my senses, pigments spinning,
starts with black, circles to white.
Make my body an instrument to measure the blues.

My Mother's Pessary *

Was she buried with it, I wonder?
That pinky-ball that for years supported
the vault over my begetting? *My fault,*
we used to joke.
Large baby, traumatic birth,
long-awaited longed-for,
late, costly.

Decades later, I witnessed
the price paid in her halting gait,
weary eyes (blue green like mine)
seeking a bench so she could sit down.
This is not like you, Mom.

Then it was I who supported
undressed, lifted. Even though
I was by then several times a mother—
I did not know this secret toll
that there could be this
late-in-life weight in the pelvis
pregnancy of years
this falling through
her overstretched muscles
falter, fail, a curtain's elasticity lost
turned inside-out like a sock.

Attended, midwife to my mother's aging
counted her breaths
an inexorable roller coaster inverted
dangles on the verge of dive-drop,
ripening
her tummy measured to house this blushing little thing
that for the last years of her life plugged up the dam
and kept the sky from falling.

Senior Citizens at the Retirement Center Discuss John Ashbery's "More Reluctant"*

I was doing okay until I got to the
wake-up call part. Is he famous, this
Ashbery? *Rambling on about*
nobody knows what—That's what
he's doing. Is all his poetry like this?
I thought there were going to be snacks.
What's that word '*spalls*?' Did anyone bring a
dictionary? Maybe it's a typo.

I think he's talking about a dream.
I like the part about *out of control*
but mature. Sometimes I feel that way.
Don't we all? What's that noise?
Lummox? What *lummox*? It's just Al,
winding the clock. No, I mean

in the poem. How old is this Ashbery guy?
I like the part where he says,
When I was young, I thought of myself as
enduring. Maybe he's visiting his home town
after being away. He says it's changed.
Moonlighters
observe customs of the spruce of the year—
It must be Christmas. Why's he talking about *pee*
all of a sudden? What's an
awful leaf and how is it *congruent*?

You brought it—*You* explain it.

Maybe it's not that
I'm stupid; maybe he's just a bad poet.
Maybe this is one of his rejects.
It was in the New Yorker. It *must* be good.
Who says? Wait. Do you think—maybe you're supposed to
not analyze it, just kind of

feel it, like
jazz?
In the last line—it's not easy
for the poet either.

My Brother and I Shared a Bathroom

Two doors faced each other. One led to his room, one to mine.
The bathroom in-between, a tunnel
through which we rattled like commuter trains
from dollhouses to Legos and back.

The bathtub a tidal pool where, once, the scandalized babysitter
caught us bathing together,
like little putti, as our mother told it.
And later, laughing with our sister, we filled blooming water balloons
from the faucet and named them *Pinky* and *Mr Green*;
we piled them in the bathtub—bright eggs in a porcelain nest
until one by one
they ruptured into nothing.

The big white pedestal sink was a summit beyond our reach.
Our mother lifted us one at a time
to hold our hands under the faucet.

Wet bathing suits hung from the rusted shower rail.
The toilet seat a toggle: He flipped it up, I thunked it down.
I traced the edges of the hexagonal tiles with bare toes,
and imagined mosaics in Pompeii.

On school mornings it was a pinball choreography,
our voices resounding on the porcelain surfaces.

In this Venn diagram,
we shared the intersection.
Always knock before you enter.
Truths glimpsed behind
the medicine cabinet door, part gossip, part mystery.
Clearasil and lotions, Tampax, shaving cream,
smells and stains and sobs.
On my side of the shared wall, I listened,
trying to match question for question,
like cards in Concentration.

Ode to a Fossil

After we stand and sigh
on the rim of the gorge
we turn our attention
to another outlook,
layer on layer on layer,
a deposition of sediment,

mudstone, siltstone, redwall,
like stacks of unread scriptures.
Older than the vista in front of us
long before anything walked on legs,
the earth buckled
uplifting an ancient sea,
a process too laborious for short-term minds.

Even the New River below us is six-million years old.
On these arid cliffs trilobites and lacy bryozoans
and gardens of fossil sea lilies high and dry,
like the petrified Pompeians,
became their own monuments.
Each empty burrow
commemorates a lifespan.

An accidental legacy,
two hundred and seventy million years ago
this dragonfly
with one beat of its lucent wings
left its mark.

Last Visit with Kathy

If she could,
she would say something funny,
pantomime some gallows humor
as once in flimsy hospital gown,
a red rose clenched between her teeth,
she raised her soft freckled arms
above her red hair
in flamenco pose.
Instead, her eyes stab like the eyes
of the chihuahua at her elbow.

Pronounce her name,
So glad to see you.

As she sips from her straw, my monologue:
Remember that time
ekphrastic writing at the museum?
The guard shuffling half-asleep
(behind his back we called him Tim Conway)
lifted a coiled extension cord
and—in the middle of your talk—
tossed it clear across the gallery.
It whizzed right past your head!
Remember when the four of us
rented that farmhouse?
Remember the crowing roosters
the goat named Ginger.
The caretaker speaking of the desk,
the chair, the table,
'That's so old," he said.
We worried he'd say the same about us.
Remember the anti-gravity chair?
We kept falling out of it,
landing on the dry August grass? We laughed
so hard.

Remember the story you told
about the mold in your bathroom—
Your mother, hard of hearing, thought it was a mole?
We laughed to tears?

That was so much fun, I say.

And is, she says.

The Middle

Feet a-dangle we skim the canopy
silent traversal, our storied leap behind.
Have we lost that once-immunity,
foolish trust in the middle of the line?
Sneaking a look at the valley's deep drop
the chance, no, certainty of grief.
What if one of us should fall—or stop—
On this zipline it is when and not if.
My ragged soul a flag in gale-force winds
everyday anniversaries strung between—
Less distant every year the upward bend
though waterfalls and anthems intervene.
Mid-freefall I choose my center of gravity—
In physics and movement I hold you close to me.

On the Subway: A Luc Bat

The sign stares back DO NOT
HOLD DOOR pressing her hot forehead
on cold metal her breath
as the doors sigh shut shirtsleeves relief
rolled up and she is hunched
around the unclosed wounds they touch
her low back, hand, thigh, brush
granite eyes transgressing on
her ribcage, her left and right lungs,
her person a stray crumb. She reads
the safety signage avidly
caught in her windpipe her voice cannot.

Attention: Ars Poetica

Hindquarters catch up with forelegs,
the rabbit sits,
nose deep in green clover
feeding on fragrance atom by atom
harelip shredding grass.
Its dark eyes, all pupil,
perceive all directions.
Ears cup and drink
rising twilight, the buzzing insects
the song of bats, barn owl shrieking.
The rabbit knows by heart
the exact distance to shelter
by frantic zigzag dash.

In this corner of the yard
generations have nibbled
summer and winter weight of padded feet.
Last season, the season before that
camouflaged in scrubby woods
taking refuge in the burrows of woodchucks.
Cycles of mating seasons, of litters, born
in scratched-out nests lined with doe's fur.
Daylight hours spent sheltering
in the shade of a hedgerow.
At dusk venturing
in search of timothy,
redtip, chickweed,
or the fare stolen from vegetable gardens
costly and rare.

The scent of night gathering.
The muffled beat of wings
this belly, this sensate air
this alfalfa blade of sweet living.

Monkey Selfie*

Once she pries it from others' grabbing,
turns it over in her hands
and mind, long black fingernails probe.
The female crested black macaque,
referencing morphology she knows she knows,
the lifted lobe, the red-fruit eyes,
she leans inward toward her vision,
welcome companion/mirror self-aware,
Snap.

Discovered in his camera's memory:
Two wide watermelon eyes,
pupils black as wells,
her superciliary arch raised
surprise? delight?
The female crested black macaque,
grinning mouthful of Chicklet teeth,
chirps her bewhiskered
orthodontic, "Cheese!"

On Watching Carla Knit

Her shoulders are still. Her anxious fingers
work the yarn into seed, rib and cable,
knitting sharp thorns in the weave of her chest.

Inside her needlecraft, the tipping of blame.
The finding of flaw, which fear does she favor?
Her shoulders are still. Her fingers

interlace, intertwine a stitch in her side,
a hook in her mouth, a hitch in her breath.
Knitting sharp thorns in the weave of her chest.

Her burden the drone beneath conversation,
wool looping around and back.
Her shoulders are still. Her fingers

fasten to patterns she fashions
and passes for love.
Knitting sharp thorns in the weave of her chest.

Pull out the knotted vine of the story.
Let it fall slack as the yarn in your lap,
Shoulders still, your worrying fingers
knit thorns in the weave of your chest.

In the Night

Scrabble of his soles heaves me from sleep.
Knees against tile, an esophagus reversed.

His gut hauls upward against will and gravity.
His cells call out inside my bloodstream,

My seasick pulse, his body dragged under.
One body, one throat catches, concedes.

Symptom of the Diagnosis

The ailment of believing you're in the wrong bathtub
The syndrome of disliking macaroni
Being convinced your face is made of glass
The sickness of being alive
The condition of rejecting honorifics
Diagnosis of listening to the rain
Phobia of being afraid
Hyper tense tension
Syndrome of syntax
Dystopia dysphoria
Humanity anxiety
Bewilderment
Calendar adjustment complaint
All-season seasonal disturbance
Hard software impairment

Died

I'd never heard the word
when, a child,
they sat me down
in the aching kitchen.
The word, a seashell,
pressed against my ear,
the crash of its sound,
the force of tides.
I pictured my grandfather
saw him *dive*
into dark water,
the man who taught me to swim
dissolved into the waves.

From the Bridge

Neera can taste water miles away
ripe mangoes, orchids, grasses
tree bark, perfume of luscious roots.

The mahouts lead them
one by one down the path
to the riverbank.
On the tips of smooth toes
elephants navigate the rocks.
Neera sways
her dusty skin dappled with brown
her magnitude is a deeply rooted thitpok tree
her backbone is a temple.

She's known logging and begging and ivory hunters
dry seasons that rise and increase.
She remembers when the herd dug for water.
Sunburned on her neck and shoulders
her leathered cheeks mapped with tears.

Picking her way down the slope
she slides into cool water and wades
wallows, falls, submerged in the bath.
Her trunk snorkels and sprays
gently rinsing her grandson's sides
washing the tender corners of his eyes.

She sees me too.
Rising awash from the river, she turns
tips her ears toward the bridge
where I watch. From the side of her head
one eye appeals.
She curls her trunk as if to mimic
the greeting known as *Wai.*

Staying Over at Mom's

Measured in teaspoons, in gravity,
in measures across sheet music,
our arm-in-arm walk
is a symphony with many movements.
I listen for her slippers on the bathmat,
the swallow of water, pills.
To be here, on the sofa-bed in the dark den,
lying awake and helpless, to help.
We cook scrambled eggs with toast
in her tiny kitchen.
I make the eggs with water, she says,
Do you? I nod, *yes.*
She says she can feel in her body
the heat and scrape of each bite of food.
Even a sip of cold water is a stab.
But these eggs are won-der-ful, she almost sings,
stretching the word like time.
How will I learn to measure her nearness
in fathoms, lightyears,
the bobby pins on her night table?
Before bed, she speaks about high school,
the Dodgers (they were in Brooklyn then),
about the West Point man she nearly married,
about my father.
She tells me just the other day a Monarch butterfly
got stuck in her window screen
and she flicked it back into flight with her finger.
I tell her about a woman I saw on the highway,
in a thunderstorm. She stopped her car
to rescue a turtle,
its wild scramble to cross
the flooded road ahead.

Sempiternam requiem

The hummingbird—a regular—
a trick of the eye—
quickened by thirst, appears.
She dips her beak
probes deeply, pulls nectar in.
Sits back like a sultan on her pillow of silken air
to savor rosewater lengthy on her tongue,
call to prayer, meditation,
just the way my mother sipped
her hot Lady Grey tea.

*

The voice first heard through water
first warmth in sudden icy light.
It's going to be all right, she told me as a child.
Sixty years later, she said the same.
Like a child that is quieted is my soul.
For the child there is no before.
But today I know,
there will be after.
As her breaths grow slow.
we read to her, a knot close enough
to hear the minutes
between inhalations,
pages of books, daylight, arias,
lifetimes of birds,
like shadows lengthened.
We read the word, *Alleluia*,
and the interval thins to infinity.

*

The twist of flight,
lift in both downbeat and upstroke,
open at any moment to complete
change of direction.

*

Her favorite chair, her reading stand, the book left open.
Woodpeckers tug at the last of the suet cake.
On a branch above,
a guardian squirrel.
And the mindful hummingbird renews her strength,
hovering, bone, heart and bill,
then mounts up,
unbound, utterly alive.

My Mother's Bobby Pins

Wearing my summer nightie
plucking the white cotton tufts
on her bedspread
I watched her
as she pinned back her hair.
The scent of Breck shampoo
her evensong ritual.
One by one she plucked them
from a china bowl
her practiced fingertips rolling the twists of hair
her wrist curling little wheels
with bobby-pin spokes.
Pinching back her brunette daytime
fullness, her face becoming
the frugal face
that appeared on slippered feet
in the night
if a voice or door
or unusual rustle was noted
on her end of the long hall.
The pinned-back nighttime
manifestation
that materialized
at my bedside.
The essence of a face spare
as a sparrow. Something—I could not
name then: Purpose,
vigil-keeping.

Object Permanence

Then, you crawled
four-legged
migrating across the floor.
Surprise! I jumped out
from behind the sofa.
Here I am!
You laughed with joy—
or was it relief?
Your hands discovered me,
handling my mouth,
tracing my ears,
fingers on my cheek.
Behind the sofa, past the corner of the room,
under the table, you found me,
you found me again and again.
We teased, we tested each other.
I out of your sight.
You out of mine.
A lesson in physics:
Objects continue to exist
even when they are not perceived.

Now, you are the one hidden
far away where I can't touch you,
can't see you.
Like a child crawling
I place my hand,
know what I know, and still doubt.

For Donation: Steinway Grand Piano

Before a bed, before a table.
The first piece of furniture my parents bought,
hand-picked by my father, selected for the hard touch
of the keys. The living room, witness
to its posture.   Excellent condition
an asset in any church or school.
And although I had many years of lessons
I could never play like him. I just don't
have space for it. Future owner:
Long after I had been tucked into bed
my father practiced
Bach   Handel   Saint-Saens
the old piano bench aching beneath him,
his soft humming,
the house and all of us,
lulled to sleep.

She Turns His Bedroom into an Office

At her desk morning and evening, in the room
        where once, folded like a hatchling swan,
the first shape he ever took, even now

she knows it, the way she knows her own voice.
        She still hears her child stalking his own four walls
disputing himself, his lecturing tone.

On his bookshelf: I Ching, Book of Myths, Book
        of The Unexplained, Charms for the Beginner.
She opens his Dictionary: Missing: A thing not able

to be found, not in its expected place. Absent.
        She sees him buying spices in a narrow street
in a time-zone seven hours ahead.

Is that the *place of tomorrow*, as Gibran said?
        Missing him is the longest night of the year.
He is teaching students in a university whose name

she can't pronounce. Pages, like weeds,
        overtake her. To miss: To fail to catch
or reach, to fail to notice or hear

or understand. To discover, feel the absence. Her own—
        She doesn't own him.
He came home from Peace Corps so thin

she thought he'd never stop eating. He came home
        from India with paint on his clothes
came home to this room, her contemplation.

Near Taksim Square, he owns the open mic,
        his gestures, his lines sweep the café
as his partner texts her, *It's OK. My mother worries too.*

Her liturgy in his paintings, his silhouette,
       certificates, clay pot. She touches each object:
Buddha, Egyptian cat, Ethiopian scroll, while he commutes

on a ferry where tea is served in tiny glasses. Missing him
       is the dervish bell she whirls in.
Missing him is its own language.

Carotenoid

Birds litter the path
with bloodied mulberries.
The apple air bites my lungs.
At the crest of the hill, the park's highest point,
I am almost there,
a mural of trees rust and russet,
hickory, poplar, sesame and sugar maple.
Just days ago this vista was green chlorophyll.
Not what the cool, lengthening night
brought, not buttercup and haystack.
I know the secret:
The colors are here
in the leaves through all seasons,
patient as my own voice
underneath the noise.
Today the green falls away,
fog dissolves,
unwraps a moon.

Notes

Letter to Marianas Trench: *"A record-setting dive to the world's most mysterious underwater trench proves even the most remote places on earth aren't immune to plastic waste,"* Daily Mail 13 May 2019

My Mother's Pessary: A therapeutic pessary is a medical device most commonly used to treat prolapse of the uterus.

Monkey Selfie: *"They were quite mischievous, jumping all over my equipment, and it looked as if they were already posing for the camera when one hit the button."*—David J. Slater, wildlife photographer

Senior Citizens at the Retirement Center Discuss John Ashbery's 'More Reluctant.' John Ashbery's poem was originally published in *The New Yorker* Feb 27 2012

Milton Keynes UK
Ingram Content Group UK Ltd.
UKHW040644101224
3563UKWH00038B/306